Easy Kids Sna
60 Snack recipes and Ideas

Family Cooking Series

by Debbie Madson

www.kids-cooking-activities.com

© Copyright 2014

All Rights Reserved, Debbie Madson

Welcome to Kids Snack Cookbook

Today snacking is a common everyday pastime. Many of us snack without even thinking what we are eating or why we are eating it. Kids snacks are important to provide energy and nourishment throughout their day. However, they want something quick and easy, which many times results in a bag of chips or whatever you have in the cupboard.

Encourage your kids to get involved in cooking. Children are naturally curious and teaching them to cook will help instill healthy eating habits, as well as encourage them to try new foods.

This cookbook is focused on:
• Involving kids in cooking activities
• Making delicious snacks that are ready in a few minutes
• Introducing new snacks for kids to try
• Using the most healthiest and natural ingredients

You'll find in the cookbook 5 basic categories including

fruit snacks
vegetable snacks
mini meals
sweet snacks
salty snacks

For a total of 60 recipes all healthy, quick and easy.

Table of Contents

Fruit Based Snacks

Kiwi Smoothie

Preparation time: 5 minutes
Yield: 2 servings

Ingredients
2 kiwis, cut in cubes
2 mint leaves
1 cup pineapple, cubed
5-6 Ice cubes, for chilling
1 cup coconut milk

Preparation
Pour all the listed ingredients in blender and combine until smooth.
Serve in two ice filled glasses
Enjoy.

Fruit Mix

Preparation time: 5 minutes
Yield: 3 servings

Ingredients
1 cup watermelons, cut in cubes
1 cup cherries
2 cups mangoes, peeled and cubed
1 cup orange juice
1 cup pineapple, cubed
1 cup apples, cut in chunks

Preparation
Take a bowl and combine all the listed ingredients in it. Serve and enjoy.

Apple and Cereal Snack Mix

Preparation time: 10 minutes
Yield 4 servings

Ingredients

4 cups cinnamon-flavored cereal, like Apple Cinnamon Cheerios
1/2 cup plain small crackers, such as oyster crackers or Goldfish
1/2 cup dried apples
1/2 cup raisins

Preparation

Mix all the listed ingredients in an airtight container.

Cream Cheese Crackers

Ingredients

4 oz cream cheese
1/4 Cup sour cream
1 tablespoon maple syrup
graham or other rectangle or square shape crackers
fresh strawberries of other fruit

Preparation

In a small bowl, blend together sour cream, cream cheese and maple syrup. Spread on cracker and top with sliced fruit.

Strawberry Smoothie

Preparation time: 5 minutes
Yield: 2 servings

Ingredients

4 oz. Fresh strawberries
2 large bananas
2 tablespoons honey
2 Cups almond milk
6 oz plain yogurt

Preparation

In a blender, combine all the ingredients until smooth.
Serve in glasses and enjoy.

A Peach of a Yogurt Cup

Ingredients
1 Cup peaches, cut into bite size pieces
8 tbsp all fruit peach spread
2 Cups of vanilla yogurt

Preparation
Place 1/4 cup of peaches into the bottom of 4 dessert glasses.
Place 2 tbsp of peach spread into each glass.
Top each glass with 1/4 Cup of yogurt.

Makes 4 servings

Apple Marshmallow Bites

Preparation time: 5 minutes
Yield: 2 servings

Ingredients
1 apple, sliced
1 cup mini marshmallows
1/2 cup Apple jam

Preparation
Place a little amount of apple jam on each apple slice.
Place the marshmallows on the apple slices.
Serve and enjoy

Fruit Smores

Ingredients

Graham cracker squares

peanut butter, nutella or cream cheese

sliced fruit, strawberries, apples, bananas, pineapple, etc.

Preparation

Prep your smores by spreading peanut butter or other spread on both sides of a graham cracker.

Place sliced fruit on a cracker square. Place graham crackers together and enjoy.

Baked Apple Slices

Preparation time: 25 minutes
Yield: 5 servings

Ingredients

5 apples, peeled
4 tablespoons orange juice
1 teaspoon cinnamon
1 tablespoon brown sugar

Preparation

Take a bowl and add cinnamon, orange juice and brown sugar in it. Set aside
Wash and peel the apples and core the center; then cut in half horizontally.
Place in baking dish and bake at 400 degree F for about 20 minutes
Once done transfer apple slices to reserved bowl with juice and other ingredients.

Banana Bites

Preparation time: 10 minutes
Yield: 2 servings

Ingredients

2 bananas, peeled
1 cup melted chocolate
1 cup nuts, crushed /and or shredded coconut

Preparation

Melt chocolate in microwave safe dish, stirring every 30 seconds until melted. Pour the nuts and/or coconut on a flat plate. Cut the bananas in half and insert a toothpick or popsicle stick in each piece. Dip them in the melted chocolate then roll it in nuts or coconut. Chill a few minutes before eating.

Freezer Pineapple Coconut Smoothies

Ingredients

1 banana
1 cup coconut milk
2 tbsp. honey
1 cup pineapple, cubed if using canned include the juice
1/3 cup coconut, pineapple or plain yogurt
2-3 ice cubes

Directions

Add all ingredients to a blender and blend until smooth. Pour into small plastic containers and freeze overnight. Let sit out several minutes until softened and eat like frozen yogurt or pack in school lunches and it will soften by lunchtime.

Cheesy Fruit

Preparation time: 5 minutes
Yield: 2 servings

Ingredients

1 apple, cut in wedges
1 pear, cut in wedges
1 cup parmesan cheese, cheddar cheese or whatever cheese your kids like

Preparation

Take a flat plate; arrange pears, apples on it. Sprinkle with cheese and place in the microwave for 30 seconds until cheese starts to melt.

If you'd like a little more to this snack serve on a English muffin and add a slice of deli ham or turkey.

Sweet Apple Dessert

Ingredients

1 crisp Gala apple
1 tbsp of sweet dried cranberries or raisins
1 tbsp of brown sugar
2 tsp of margarine
1/2 C of granola or dried cereal

Preparation

Core apple and cut in half. Place in a microwave safe bowl. Sprinkle each half with cranberries and brown sugar. Place 1 tsp of margarine onto each apple half. Cover with plastic wrap or parchment paper and microwave for 2-3 minutes or until apple is soft. Sprinkle with the granola before serving.

Berries Yogurt Parfait

Preparation time: 5 minutes
Yield: 2 servings

Ingredients
1 cup strawberries, blueberries or blackberries or combination
1 cup Greek yogurt
granola or dried cereal your kids like

Preparation
Layer in a serving cup, berries, yogurt, granola and more berries.

Blueberry Gummy Fruit Snacks

Preparation time: 5 minutes
Yield: 2 servings

Ingredients
2 cups blueberries
1/2 cup water
1 cup applesauce
1 cup apple juice
5 teaspoons gelatin, 2 envelopes

Preparation
Grease a 13x9 baking dish and set aside. In a pan cook berries and water. Once the mixture starts to boil, cooking for an additional 3-5 minutes. Pour into blender and puree. Add back to pan and mix in applesauce. Meanwhile, sprinkle gelatin in fruit juice and add in to pan. Cook until starts to thicken. Pour mixture into baking dish and chill for about 3 to 4 hours until solid. Cut into desirable shapes and enjoy.

Strawberry Bites

Ingredients
4 (6 in) soft tortilla shells
1/4 (8 oz) container strawberry cream cheese*
4 Tablespoons strawberry jam

Preparation
Spread each of the 4 tortillas with the strawberry cream cheese to the edges of the tortilla.
Spread 1 T of strawberry jam down the middle of each of the tortillas.
Fold the end of the tortilla in about 2 in.
Grab the front edge of the tortilla and roll until completely closed.
Cut into 2 inch bites.

Serving Size: 24
*If you don't have strawberry cream cheese use plain with the strawberry jam instead.

Fruit Kabobs

It's a simple idea but one kids love. Giving kids the chance to pick and choose what they want gives them more responsibility and builds confidence.

Preparation

Place a variety of fresh fruit on a plate and let kids arrange their own fruit kabob. Depending on how much fruit you have available, I like to tell kids to pick at least three different kinds.

Creamy Cinnamon Applesauce Dip

Ingredients

2 Cups applesauce
6 Tablespoons of vanilla yogurt
1 teaspoon ground cinnamon

Preparation

Place the applesauce into a serving bowl.
Fold in the yogurt until well combined.
Sprinkle in the cinnamon and stir until blended in well.
Cover tightly and refrigerate for at least 30 minutes
before serving.

Choose your favorite dunkers such as animal
crackers, graham crackers, vanilla wafer or lightly
frosted shredded wheat cereal.

Hawaiian Fruit Dip

Ingredients

1 (3.4 oz) package Instant Vanilla Pudding Mix
1 1/4 cup cold milk
1/2 cup sour cream
1 (8 oz) can crushed pineapple, undrained
1/3 cup shredded coconut
fresh fruit for dipping – melon, apple, strawberries, kiwi, orange, peach, mango, papaya

Preparation

In a large bowl, put the pudding mix and milk and whisk together until smooth, then add the sour cream and whisk to combine. With a spoon, stir in the pineapple, with the juice, and the coconut.
Cover and put in refrigerator for at least an hour.
Serve cold alongside fresh fruit for dipping.

Creamy Fruit Dip

Ingredients
1/2 Cup of pineapple cream cheese, softened*
2 (8 oz.) containers of lemon yogurt
1/2 Cup of dried mixed fruit, apricots, raisins, chopped apples or craisins all work great
dippers, fruit slices, graham crackers, pita chips

Preparation
Place the cream cheese into a serving bowl.
Add the lemon yogurt and mix with an electric mixer on low speed until smooth.
Fold in the dried mixed fruit.
Cover the bowl tightly and chill for at least 1 hour.

Makes 8 servings
*If you don't have pineapple cream cheese available, mix 1/2 Cup cream cheese with 1/4 Cup crushed pineapple

Vegetable Snacks

Kale Chips

Preparation time: 20 minutes
Yield: 2 servings

Ingredients
1 bunch Kale
1 Tablespoon olive oil
1/2 cup parmesan cheese
Pinch of salt and pepper

Preparation
Wash and tear the kale leaves off the stems.
Let them dry and place on a cookie sheet. Drizzle with
olive oil and sprinkle with parmesan cheese., salt and
pepper. Bake in oven at 375 degree F for about 15
minutes until leaves get crunchy.

Mashed Potato Stuffed Mushrooms

Cooking time: 20 minutes
Yield 4 servings

Ingredients
2 potatoes, boiled and mashed or 1-2 Cups instant mashed potatoes
2 Cups whole mushrooms
pinch of salt and black pepper
1/2 Cup cottage cheese

Preparation
Remove stems from mushrooms. In a bowl, mix mashed potatoes, salt, cheese and pepper. Fill mixture in caps of mushrooms.
Bake in oven at 375 degree F for about 10-15 minutes. Serve and enjoy.

Chicken Stuffed Eggplants

Preparation time: 10 minutes
Yield: 2 servings

Ingredients

2-3 small-medium eggplants, center cored
1 onion, diced
1/2 teaspoons salt
1 garlic clove
1 teaspoons ginger, paste
5 tablespoons olive oil
1 cup cheddar cheese, shredded
1 cup chicken, shredded

Preparation

Cut eggplants in half and scoop out the inside to make a boat. In a skillet, sauté onions in olive oil. Then stir in garlic and ginger. Add chicken and cook an additional 15 minutes.

Add cooked ingredients to a bowl and mix in cheddar cheese. Add the mixture into each eggplant boat. Bake at 375 Degrees for 10 minutes or until soft.

Cookie Cutter Veggie Bites

Ingredients

pie crusts, homemade or store bought
8 oz cream cheese, softened at room temp
1 Tablespoon milk
dash of Worcestershire sauce
variety of vegetables cut in small pieces , tomatoes, cucumbers, radish, broccoli, carrots, etc- whatever you like to eat.
cookie cutters

Preparation

Using cookie cutters, cut different shapes out of pie crust and place on a cookie sheet. Preheat oven to 425 degrees.

With a fork, pierce each pie crust several times. Bake pie crusts for 5-7 minutes until golden brown. Let cool off

In small bowl, blend together cream cheese, 1 Tablespoon milk and a dash of Worcestershire sauce. Blend together. Spread mixture on pie crust shapes. Top with an arrangement of chopped vegetables.

~Let the kids have some fun helping with these. Use whatever veggies you like and their imagination.

Sweetened Shredded Carrot and Nuts

Preparation time: 15 minutes
Yield: 2 servings

Ingredients
4 Cups Carrots, shredded and boiled
2 Cups milk
5 tablespoons butter
2 cups brown sugar
1 Cup nuts for garnishing (optional)

Preparation
In saucepan, heat milk and add shredded carrots.
Cook about 10 minutes. Milk will evaporate. Pour in
the butter and sugar and cook an additional 10
minutes. Toss with nuts before serving.

Cheesy Potatoes Balls

Preparation time: 25 minutes
Yield: 4 servings

Ingredients

2 potatoes, boiled and peeled
2 Cups cottage cheese
1 Cup mushrooms, diced
1 Cup shredded chicken, boiled
Salt and pepper, to taste
1 Cup bread crumbs
Olive oil for deep-frying

Preparation

In a bowl, combine together boiled potatoes, cottage cheese, mushrooms, chicken, salt and pepper. Mix well and then form into small balls. Roll balls in breadcrumbs. Chill while oil warms up. In a wok or skillet, heat olive oil. Fry the potato balls until brown. Serve with sour cream for dipping.

Sweet Potato Wedges

Preparation time: 15 minutes
Yield: 2 servings

Ingredients
2 large sweet potatoes, cut into wedges
1/2 teaspoon cumin
1/3 teaspoon of paprika
2 tablespoons olive oil
1/2 teaspoon salt
Dash of cayenne pepper

Preparation
Preheat oven at 400 degree F. In a bowl, mix all the listed ingredients. Once the sweet potatoes are coated, grease a baking dish with oil and place potato wedges on top. Bake in oven for about 15-20 minutes until tender. Serve with ketchup.

Vegetable Stick People

Ingredients

variety of vegetables cut in slices, small pieces, circles, etc

Preparation

Let kids practice their creativity and have fun eating what they create. Use your cut vegetables to design your own stick people. Serve with salad dressing for dipping if you'd like.

Onion Rings

Preparation time: 25 minutes
Yield: 4 servings

Ingredients
4 Onions, cut in rings
1 Cup bread crumbs
2 eggs, whisked

Preparation
Cut onion in rings and dip in beaten eggs. Dip rings in breadcrumbs and lay on a greased baking sheet. Bake at 350 degrees F for 20 minutes or until crispy. Serve.

Cucumber Boats

Preparation

Cut a large cucumber in half and scoop out insides. Fill with tuna salad, chicken salad, whatever you'd like. We filled ours with a Greek salad and added flags for fun. Perhaps we should have added a Greek flag but didn't have one!

Pumpkin Dip

Ingredients

1 (15 oz) can prepared pumpkin
1 tsp. cinnamon
1/4 Cup pecans, finely chopped
1 (4 oz) pkg. cream cheese, softened
Graham crackers

Preparation

Blend together pumpkin, cinnamon and cream cheese until well blended. Stir in pecans and serve with graham crackers.

Spinach Dip

Ingredients

1 Cup light mayonnaise
1 Cup light sour cream
1 (10 oz) pkg. frozen spinach, thawed and chopped
1 envelope dry vegetable soup mix
1 loaf of French bread or crackers

Preparation

Unthaw spinach and place between paper towels. Squeeze water out of spinach. Blend together mayonnaise, sour cream, vegetable soup mix and chopped spinach until well combined. Chill several hours and serve with sliced French bread or crackers.

Carrot Fries

Ingredients
12 carrots
2 Tablespoons olive oil
Sea salt to taste
dash of cayenne pepper

Preparation
Wash, peel and cut carrots into strips. Place on cookie sheet and drizzle olive oil. Toss to coat. Sprinkle with salt and cayenne pepper. Toss again until all carrots have seasoning. Bake at 400 degrees for 15-20 minutes until light brown.
~If your kids don't like spicy try cinnamon sugar mixture instead of cayenne pepper and salt.

Baked Chip Dip

Ingredients
1 Cup fat free refried beans
2/3 Cup salsa
1 bag of baked potato chips or tortilla chips

Preparation
Place the beans in a mixing bowl.
Add the salsa and stir to combine.
Serve with baked chips.

Tuna Lettuce Warp

Ingredients
Lettuce leaf
small can of tuna
1 Tablespoons mayonnaise
1 Tablespoon chopped pickles or pickle relish

Preparation
Drain tuna and add into a bowl. Blend in mayonnaise and pickles. Stir until well combined. Add spoonfuls of tuna mixture onto a lettuce leaf. Wrap up and enjoy! Makes about 2-3 servings depending on size of leaves

Mini Meal Snacks

Cabbage and Salmon Snack
Preparation time: 10 minutes
Yield: 2 servings

Ingredients
2 leaves of cabbage
4 oz. smoked salmon
1 red onion, minced
1 avocado, slice
Salt and black pepper to taste
olive or coconut oil for drizzling

Preparation
Wash the cabbage and separate the leaves. On a
large leaf, add salmon, avocado slice and onion.
Sprinkle salt and pepper at the end. Drizzle oil just
before serving

Deviled Eggs Boats

Ingredients

1 dozen hard boiled eggs, peeled, washed and split in half
1/2 Cup mayonnaise
1 tbsp mustard
1 Tablespoon chopped pickles or celery
Green or red peppers cut in triangles

Preparation

Prepare eggs as stated above. Take yolk out of each egg and place in a bowl. Add mayonnaise, mustard and chopped pickles. Blend together until well combined and yolks are broken in small pieces. Fill each egg half with yolk mix. Sprinkle with a little paprika before eating.
~Add a pepper cut into a triangle for a sailboat.

Stuffed Dates

Cooking time: 5 minutes

Ingredients
8-10 dates, pitted and cut in half lengthwise
1 Can sweetened condensed milk
8 oz cream cheese
1/2 Cup cottage cheese
4-tablespoon orange juice
1/2 Cup almonds, chopped

Preparation
In a bowl, combine cottage cheese, cream cheese and condensed milk. Blend in orange juice, and almonds. stir until well combined and fill pitted dates with mixture.

Mozzarella Nibblers

Ingredients
3 Tablespoons of flour
1/2 teaspoon of salt
1/4 teaspoon of pepper
1 egg
1 teaspoon water
1 1/2 Cups of fresh bread crumbs
1 (8 oz.) block of mozzarella cheese, cubed
Canola oil

Preparation
Place the flour, salt and pepper into a zip lock baggie. Break the egg into a small bowl.
Blend water into egg and whisk until combined. Place the bread crumbs into a shallow bowl. Add oil in pan, wok or deep fryer, heat.
Place a few cheese cubes into the flour mixture and shake to coat. Then dip the coated cheese cubes into the egg mixture shaking off any excess egg. Roll each cheese cube through the bread crumbs to lightly coat on all sides. Drop the coated cheese cubed into the hot oil.
Fry 2 minutes, turning occasionally. Cook until the cheese begins to melt and the outside is a crispy golden brown. Drain the cheese cubes on paper towel before serving.
Makes 8 servings

~Do you want a healthy snack? Lay coated cheese cubes on a cookie sheet. Spray with cooking spray and bake at 450 degrees until crispy.

Pesto Pizza Bread

Cooking time: 15 minutes
Yield : 1 serving

Ingredients
2 French bread pieces
1 Cup pesto sauce
1/2 cup shredded Parmesan
1thin-sliced tomato
1 cup back olives
1/2 cup mozzarella
1 cup mushrooms , chopped

Preparation
In a bowl, mix together pesto, black olives,
mushrooms, shredded parmesan and mozzarella.
Once combined pour this on bread slices and top with
tomato slices. Bake in oven at 350 degree F, for
about 10 minutes until cheese melts.
~If kids prefer use marinara sauce in place of pesto
sauce

Taco Quesadilla

Ingredients
1/2 Cup kidney beans or refried beans
cooked ground beef, optional
spoonful of salsa, however much you like
1/4 Cup shredded cheese
2 tortillas

Preparation
On a tortilla spread beans and sprinkle with cooked hamburger. Spread salsa and cheese over the top. Place another tortilla on the top and fry in a skillet or bake in a 400 degree oven until golden brown.

~Mix and change whichever ingredients you like such as, chicken in place of hamburger or add chopped olives.

Chicken Peanut Ramen Noodles

Preparation time: 10 minutes
Yield 3 servings

Ingredients
1 packet instant chicken Ramen noodles
rotisserie chicken, shredded
1/2 tablespoon soy sauce
handful of peanuts
dash of hot sauce, if desired

Preparation
Cook Ramen noodles according to package directions using flavor packet as well. Drain noodles and toss in shredded chicken, soy sauce and peanuts. If you like spicy add a small dash of hot sauce.

Cheesy Asparagus Topped Crackers

Ingredients
12 asparagus spears
1 Tablespoon water
cream cheese flavored with herbs, softened
Parmesan cheese, shredded
Crackers

Preparation
Snap ends off asparagus and throw ends away. Snap rest of asparagus spears into 1 inch pieces and place in a microwave safe bowl. Add the water and cover. Microwave for 4 minutes or until the asparagus is fork tender. Drain off any excess water.
 Spread the cream cheese on the crackers. Sprinkle with Parmesan cheese. Top with the asparagus pieces.

**If you'd rather use a different vegetable then asparagus try cucumbers cut in slices or steamed broccoli spears.

Sweet Snacks

Yogurt Popsicle

Yield : 6-8 serving
Freeze overnight
Ingredients

4 small ripe bananas
1 cup frozen blueberries or raspberries
4 cups non-fat plain yogurt
4 tablespoons honey

Preparation

Combine all the ingredients in blender and once
puree, pour into Popsicle molds
Freeze overnight and then serve.

Chocolate Snack Mix

Cooking time: 5minutes
Yield : 4 serving

Ingredients
4 cups of square-shaped corn cereals (such as Chex)
1/2 Cup chocolate chips
1Cup peanut butter
1/2 Cup brown sugar
1/4 teaspoon vanilla

Preparation

Combine chocolate chips, butter, sugar and vanilla in a bowl and microwave for about a minute. Add the cereal to a large bowl. Pour the melted mixture over the cereals, stir until all is coated.

Coconut Cookies

Cooking time: 20 minutes
Yield: 4 serving

Ingredients
1 Cup coconut flour
1 Cup white flour
1/2 Cup butter
1 Cup sugar
2 eggs
1 teaspoon baking soda
1/4 cup cream of coconut
chopped almonds and/or mini chocolate chips
1 Cup shredded coconut

Preparation
Preheat oven at 375 degree F.
In a bowl, combine eggs with sugar.
In another bowl, combine baking powder, white flour, coconut flour, cream of coconut and coconut milk. Stir in coconut and nut or chips.
Spray the baking sheet with cooking spray and place spoonfuls of mixture onto the pan. Bake in oven for about 10-12 minutes or until lightly golden brown.

Banana Muffins

Preparation time: 25 minutes
Yield: 8-10 servings

Ingredients
1 1/2 Cups sugar
3/4 Cup butter, softened
4 eggs
4 mashed bananas
1/2 teaspoon soda
3 1/2 Cups flour
1 teaspoon salt
1 teaspoon vanilla
1 Cup walnuts (optional)

Preparation
Preheat oven at 350 degree F. Line muffin tin with muffin paper cups. In a mixing bowl, cream together sugar and butter until creamy. Add in eggs, bananas and vanilla, blend. Add in the flour, soda, and salt. Continue blend until well combined. Stir in walnuts if desired. Scoop batter into muffin cups and bake for about 15 minutes until lightly golden brown.

Banana PB & Chocolate Ice Cream

Preparation time: 10 minutes
Cooking time: 1 minute
Freeze in refrigerator over night
Yield 2 servings

Ingredients

1 Tablespoon cocoa powder
3 Tablespoons peanut butter
4 bananas, peeled, broken in pieces

Preparation

In a food processor, combine all the ingredients and
blend one minute or until smooth.
Pour the mixture in a plastic container and freeze,
preferably overnight.

Blueberry Waffle

Cooking time: 15 minutes
Yield : 4 serving

Ingredients
1 cup milk
2 cups all-purpose flour
1teaspoons baking powder
2 Cups fresh or frozen blueberries, rinsed
3 eggs, separated
1 Cup melted butter
5 Tablespoons sugar

Preparation
Beat the eggs until they become fluffy. Next in separate bowl, beat egg yolks and blend in the butter and milk. Mix in all the remaining ingredients, except blueberries. Gently stir in the beaten egg whites and blueberries. Add a scoop of batter onto a hot waffle iron. Cook until crispy.

5 minute Granola Balls

Ingredients
1 Cup plain rolled oats
4 Tablespoons flax seed
1 Tablespoon honey
1 Tablespoon peanut butter
1/4 Cup raisins
2 Tablespoons milk
1/2 Cup shredded coconut

Preparation
In food processor, blend granola and raisin until finely chopped. Stir in flax seed, honey and peanut butter. Pulse a few times to combine. If mixture is too dry to form into balls add in 1 Tablespoon of milk at a time until good consistency. Roll balls and then roll into shredded coconut.

Jam Twists

Ingredients
puff pastry
1/2 jam of choice

Preparation
Preheat oven at 350 degrees. Lay a sheet of puff pastry flat and spread all over with jam. Lay another sheet of pastry on top of the jam. Cut into strips.

Fold a strip in half making a loop. Twist together. Place on cookie sheet. Continue with all the puff pastry strips. Bake for 15-20 minutes until golden brown.

Fruit Pizza Rice Cake

Ingredients
1 rice cake
Nutella spread or peanut butter
strawberry and/or banana, cut in slices
mini chocolate chips or chopped nuts, optional

Preparation
Spread Nutella over a rice cake and top with sliced
fruit. If desired, add a little topping like chopped nuts
or mini chocolate chips

Banana Fritters

Cooking time: 10 minutes
Yield 2 servings

Ingredients
2 bananas, peeled and sliced lengthwise
4 egg roll wrappers papers
Pinch of cinnamon
2 tablespoons sugar
1/2 cup Canola oil for frying
2 tablespoons honey, for drizzling on top

Preparation
Coat the banana slices with sugar and cinnamon.
Place the egg roll wrapper on a flat surface and
arrange 2 banana slices in the middle.
Roll up, tucking in the sides. Dip your finger in water
and wet the ends of the wrapper to keep the end for
unfolding.
Warm a small pan with oil. Fry rolls in oil until golden
brown.

If you'd rather cook in oven, place banana rolls on a
cookie sheet and spray with cooking spray. Bake at
450 degrees until crispy. They won't be quite the
same as fried, but healthier.
Serve by drizzling honey on top.

Salty Snacks

Taco Mexican Mix

Ingredients

3 Cups baked cheese crackers or goldfish crackers
2 Cups butter flavored pretzel sticks
1 Cup rice Chex cereal
1 Cup of peanuts
1 Tablespoon of vegetable oil
2 Tablespoons dry taco seasoning mix

Preparation

Place the crackers in a large microwave safe mixing bowl.

Add the pretzels and peanuts and gently toss to combine.

Drizzle the oil over the top and stir with a spoon to evenly coat.

Sprinkle with the taco seasoning mix and stir again to coat well.

Microwave the mixture on high for 2 minutes.

Remove and stir with a wooden spoon.

Return to the microwave and heat for an additional 2 minutes on high.

Allow the mix to stand 5 minutes before serving.

Homemade Crackers

Ingredients

1 lb. Cheddar cheese, shredded or Colby or a combination of both
1 Cup butter, soft cut in cubes
1/4 Cup sugar
1 1/2 Cups white flour
1 1/2 Cups wheat flour
1/2 Cup milk
2 tsp salt
1 tsp. cayenne pepper

Preparation

Place the cheese, cayenne pepper, salt and butter into a large mixing bowl. Cream together. Blend in sugar, milk and flours. Keep mixing the ingredients until a soft dough forms. Shape the dough into a single log. Chill in the refrigerator until firm. Heat the oven to 375 degrees. Remove the dough roll and place on a flat surface. Slice the roll into thin slices. Place the slices on an ungreased baking sheet. Bake 8 minutes or until crispy.
~Experiment with different seasonings, Italian herb mix in place of cayenne pepper or
~For fun you can roll the dough out and cut with cookie cutters, as well.

Mix it UP Tortilla Chips

Ingredients
2 flour tortillas
2 corn tortillas
2 sun-dried tomato tortillas
2 spinach tortillas
Nonstick cooking spray
salt
garlic salt
onion salt
chili powder

Preparation
Preheat oven to 400 degrees. Put tortillas on clean surface and spray with cooking spray, then sprinkle with seasonings to your taste. Flip over, spray and season the other side. Pile the tortillas up on a cutting board and cut into quarters using a sharp knife, forming 4 triangles. Put the cut tortillas on baking sheets being sure not to overlap any.
Bake in preheated oven until crisp, about 5 to 7 minutes. Remove from oven and slide off onto a cooling rack. They will get crispier as they cool.

Seasoned Crackers

10 cups oyster crackers or plain goldfish crackers
1/2 cup vegetable oil
1/2 tsp garlic salt
1/2 tsp dried thyme
1/2 tsp dried oregano
1/4 tsp cumin
1/4 tsp paprika

Put oyster crackers in large bowl and drizzle with oil, tossing to coat evenly.
Put oyster crackers in large paper bag and add seasonings, then shake vigorously to coat the crackers with seasonings.
Store in an airtight container.
You can eat these as a snack or add them to soups and salads.

Toasted Pumpkin Seeds

Ingredients
1 qt. water
2 Tablespoons salt
2 Cups fresh pumpkin seeds*
1 Tablespoons unsalted butter, melted

Preparation
Place the oven temperature on 250 degrees
Place the water in a large saucepan over medium high heat.
Sprinkle in the salt and bring the water to a steady boil.
Add the seeds and continue boiling for 12 minutes.
Drain the seeds well using a colander.
 *If using packaged pumpkin seeds skip the above steps.
Lay the seeds in a single layer on a piece of paper towel and pat them dry.
Place the melted butter in a mixing bowl.
Add the seeds and toss to coat evenly.
Spread the seeds in a single layer on a large baking sheet.
Bake 35 minutes being sure to stir every 12 minutes or so during the baking. Seeds should be a light golden brown and crispy when toasted.
Allow the seeds to cool before shelling and eating.

Microwave Cheese Almonds

Ingredients
1 tbsp butter, softened
1/2 Cup of sharp cheddar cheese, shredded
1/4 Cup of flour
1 dash cayenne pepper
small pkg. hickory smoked almonds or plain almonds

Preparation
Mix the butter and cheese together until smooth.
Add the flour, cayenne pepper and celery seed and
knead until the mixture forms a ball. If mixture is too
dry add 1 teaspoon or less of water until mixture
forms a ball.
Place a teaspoonful of the cheese dough around each
almond to completely cover the almond.
Place the covered almonds into a circle of 9 on 4
microwave safe plates.
Microwave the cheese almonds on high for 2 minutes,
rotating the plate a quarter turn after 1 minute.

*The cheese dough will not hold it shape but will be
slightly dry and puffy when done.*
Repeat until all the cheese almonds have been
cooked.
Allow to cool slightly before serving.

Maple and Spice Snack Mix

Ingredients

1/4 Cup sugar free pancake syrup
2 tbsp unsalted butter, cut up in small chunks
1 tbsp chili powder
1/2 tsp salt
1/4 tsp cinnamon
3 Cups air popped popcorn
3 Cups mixed nuts, unsalted
1 Cup wheat nuts or wheat germ
1/3 Cup dried blueberries or other dried fruit

Preparation

Pour the syrup into a medium size saucepan. Place over low heat. Add the butter and let it begin to melt. Sprinkle in the chili powder, salt and cinnamon. Stirring often continue to cook on low until the butter has completely melted.

Set the oven temperature to 300 degrees.

Toss together the popcorn, mixed nuts, wheat nuts and blueberries in a large baking pan. Pour the syrup mixture over the top and toss to coat all the ingredients completely.

Bake 25 minutes or until golden brown. Be sure to stir the snack mix a couple of times during baking to ensure it browns evenly.

Cool the snack mix to room temperature before storing in a container.

17197392R10039

Made in the USA
Middletown, DE
11 January 2015